T0272876

THE SKETCHBOOK OF A GENTLEMAN

TUSCANY · ROBIN LUCAS

COLLECTIVE SHORTS
by NHP PUBLISHING

To my parents

The Sketchbook of a Gentleman – Tuscany

Italy has a long and intimate relationship with art. Some of the greatest artists in history hail from Italy and their work can been seen in every part of Italian life, from its majestic churches to virtuoso architecture. The hill towns of the Val d'Orcia, and the world famous cities of Florence and Siena, are the very epitome of this heady cultural mix.

Famously, food and family are also integral to Italian life, with recipes and cultural heritage being passed down through generations. Every region of Italy has a deep pride in its food and wine; Tuscany is no exception. Sometimes even the most familiar road can yield hidden gems; private houses, gardens, and Osterias tucked away in ancient villages.

This book is the second instalment of Edward's illustrated travels, where, ever the gentleman, he journeys through the heart of Tuscany enjoying all aspects of that privileged region.

Monday

Ciao Firenze

One can escape London,

but apparently not the crowds

Via Tornabuoni 64/r 50123

Many choices,
but the truffle panini
is the only thing to have!

Raising the bar

The Primi Sali
- Tratoria Cammillo

Tagliolini con prosciutto e piselli

Buona notte

And so to bed

Tuesday

The most important meal of the day

The Harold
Acton Library

Time to catch up

A light lunch today

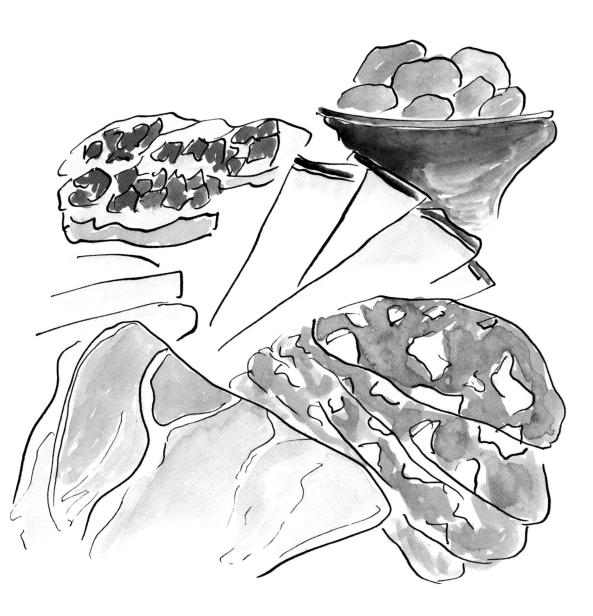

'You will begin to wonder that human daring ever achieved anything so magnificent.' Ruskin

Too heavy for my luggage

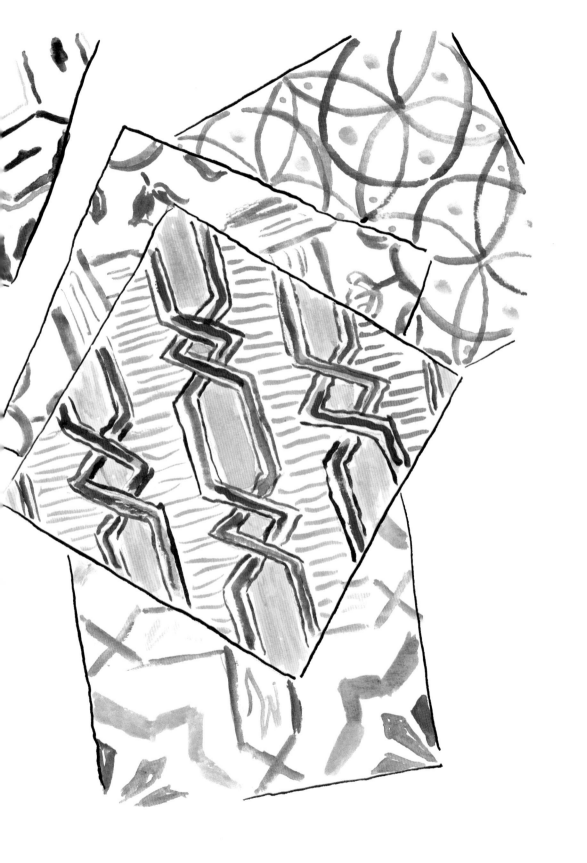

He's a great travel companion

but no so great with maps

Wednesday

Waking up at Arniano

Six centuries later, and still standing ...

... just

A warm welcome at La Bandita Townhouse

Fiori di zucca

'Images and Shadows' at La Foce

Cecil Pinsent's garden for Iris Origo

- a true masterpiece

Via del Piano, 1, Monticcihello

Ice, equal prosecco and Aperol with a dash of
soda and a slice of orange

A post dinner saunter

Thursday

Never trust a café without regulars!

The Sodoma frescos,
Abbazia Monte Oliveto Maggiore

Why not judge a book by it's cover?

It would be foolish not to!

Like Nonna made it

Perfection !

He makes a cracking Martini

Friday

Nothing sour about this trip!

'The Hostess with the Mostess'

What's cooking?

Finocchio

Time to move on

Via del Porrione, Siena

Never alone in Siena

35 ml Tanqueray
25 ml Campari
25 ml Martini Rosso
Blend with a twist

Saturday

I must come back for the Palio!

When in Italy...

A perfect spot for people watching

The Contrade of Siena

Towards the Duomo

The colours of Siena

Villa Cetinale - hard to think of a better place
for a party

The promise of good things to come

It's the taking part that counts

Sunday

A very slow start

Breakfast in the loggia

No dogs on the sofa (except this one)

Gamberi

A few loops

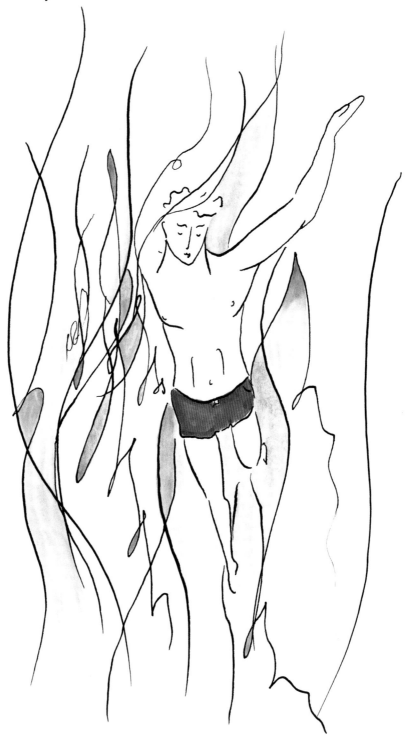

Much refreshed!

THE SKETCHBOOK
OF A GENTLEMAN
TUSCANY · ROBIN LUCAS

Published by New Heroes & Pioneers
Illustrations and text: Robin Lucas
Creative Direction: Francois Le Bled
Book Design: Daniel Zachrisson
Copy Editing: Matt Porter

Printed and bound by Balto print (Lithuania)
Legal deposit November 2018
ISBN 978-91-87815-27-0

"I would like to thank Amber Guinness and Matthew Bell, also
Emily Fitzroy all without whom this book wouldn't have been possible.
A very warm thanks also to all those in Tuscany who welcomed me,
over the years, to their homes, gardens, and businesses. I would also
like to thank my family and partner for their unwavering support."
– Robin Lucas

COLLECTIVE SHORTS
by NHP PUBLISHING